Alexander McCaul

An examination of Bp. Colenso's difficulties with regard to the Pentateuch

Part II

Alexander McCaul

An examination of Bp. Colenso's difficulties with regard to the Pentateuch
Part II

ISBN/EAN: 9783337131388

Printed in Europe, USA, Canada, Australia, Japan

Cover: Foto ©Lupo / pixelio.de

More available books at **www.hansebooks.com**

AN EXAMINATION

OF

BP. COLENSO'S DIFFICULTIES

WITH REGARD TO

THE PENTATEUCH

PART II.

BY THE REV.

ALEXANDER McCAUL,

LATE PROFESSOR OF HEBREW AND OLD TESTAMENT
KING'S COLLEGE, LONDON.

LONDON;
RIVINGTONS, WATERLOO PLACE:
AND HIGH STREET, OXFORD.
1864.

LONDON
GILBERT AND RIVINGTON, PRINTERS,
ST. JOHN'S SQUARE.

PREFACE.

THE substance of the following pages was delivered as Lectures during Dr. McCaul's last Term at King's College. The commencement and a portion of the conclusion he re-wrote for publication. Had he lived, the remainder also would doubtless have been enriched with notes and references. His last effort in defence of God's truth, it will possess a melancholy interest for his friends; even from those who differ from him, his learning and his originality of thought will, I trust, ensure for it a patient consideration.

The abbreviation D. C., of the first Part, has been retained.

A. I. McC.

Rectory, London Bridge,
February 1, 1864.

EXAMINATION,

&c.

PART II.

—— — ——

In the first part of Bishop Colenso's " Examination of the Pentateuch and Joshua " there was
but little of philological criticism. The objections were generally popular, and easily under-
stood by all who read English. In the second
part, notwithstanding a strenuous effort to make
his argument equally perspicuous, a great deal
must appear uncertain to those who are not
familiar with the Hebrew original, and must
necessarily, if received at all, be taken upon
trust upon the mere assertion of Bishop Colenso
himself. In answering this second part therefore it will be necessary not only to show the
invalidity of arguments, but to compare autho-
rities. D. C. is not the first nor the only critic
in the world who has propounded a theory of
the Pentateuch similar to his. In the first part
his object was to prove that the Pentateuch is

B

unhistoric: in the second, to show that it was not written by Moses. To show that Moses was not the author, he asserts first, that the Pentateuch, or a portion of it, is made up of two documents distinguished by the peculiar use of the two words, Elohim, *God*, and Jehovah, LORD, written by two different authors, the Elohist, and the Jehovist,—both living long after the time of Moses; the former being Samuel, and the latter some one who lived later still. Our first business must therefore be to examine the proofs on which his assertion rests that the Pentateuch is composed of two documents, and that these were written by two different authors. That it might be composed of two or of twenty documents is possible without in any degree diminishing from its credibility. Histories written long after the events must, in order to be trustworthy, necessarily derive their materials from older works:—and the older the materials, and the greater the diligence in using them, the more trustworthy is the history compiled from them. Thus if Moses wrote the Book of Genesis, containing an account of the fall of man, of the antediluvian world, the deluge, and the call of Abraham, it is possible that he might have ancient documents, written by Adam, Seth, Noah, Abraham, and others; and that the Spirit guided him to select those parts which he has incorporated into his own narrative: and therefore Vitringa and other Christian men have conjectured the fact of such compilation. Could this be proved, it would of course make the Mosaic narrative not less trustworthy, and more interesting.

The mere fact, therefore, of a variety of documents going to make up the narrative of Moses would of itself in no wise affect the authenticity of the history. But may we trust Bishop Colenso when he says that the documents are two, and writers two? Is this the general opinion of the great Biblical scholars, who have investigated the subject for the last hundred years?—Astruc, who first propounded a distinct theory on the subject, taught that the Book of Genesis is made up of twelve memoirs or documents, of which the Elohistic and the Jehovistic are only the principal. Eichhorn indeed asserted that Genesis is based upon two documents; but he affirmed that they were both pre-Mosaic, and that some other documents were consulted. Ilgen supposed seventeen documents, and three authors; one Jehovist and two Elohists. De Wette maintains one Elohistic and several Jehovistic documents. Von Bohlen believes in the same Elohistic basis, but denies any Jehovistic document: the compiler is the Jehovist. Gramberg makes three authors, the Elohist, the Jehovist, and the compiler. Ewald has varied in his statements: first, holding the unity of Genesis: then, an Elohistic document, founded on more ancient writings: then, the present Book of Genesis founded on six similar preceding works, of which three were Elohistic. Hupfeld takes as the basis of our book of Genesis three independent historic works; two Elohistic, one Jehovistic, and makes a compiler besides. Knobel makes an Elohistic basis, compounded with a Jehovistic founded on two previous documents, and then tradition and the contributions of the compiler himself. Hengstenberg, Hävernick, Kurtz, Kiel, &c., affirm that the whole was written by Moses. Now here is a great variety of opinions. To which of the authors should the English reader give his confidence? To Bishop Colenso, who began this sort of study two years ago, or to one of those great German scholars who have passed their lives in studying the criticisms of others or criticizing themselves? or where there is such great difference of opinion, will he give his confidence to any? Will he adopt the dictum of Colenso, who says there are two writers, or of Ilgen, who makes three, or Hupfeld and Knobel, who make four, or of Ewald, who in his latest affirmation makes seven? Will the unlearned reader accept one Elohist with Colenso and Knobel? or with Ilgen and Hupfeld two? or with Ewald three? and with his one, two, or three Elohists does he choose to join one, two, or more Jehovistic writers? It is evident that all these learned critics cannot be right; they may all be wrong. The whole Jewish nation believe, and have believed them wrong, so far as their faith can be traced: Christian scholars until one hundred years ago, many of them profound Hebraists, have believed them wrong: many learned critics of the present day, quite equal in learning, think them wrong. These critics themselves think one another wrong. De Wette rejects Ilgen: Hupfeld rejects De Wette: Knobel rejects Hupfeld: Ewald rejects the foregoing, and D. C. rejects all these geniuses alike.

[To ask us to believe in such criticism is perfectly ludicrous, especially when we know the outspoken manner in which some of these critics charge each other with ignorance and incompetence. . Two of the most celebrated of these now living are Ewald and Hupfeld. Let us hear what they think of each other as critics. Hupfeld wrote in a German periodical, and subsequently published, separately, " The sources of the Book of Genesis, and the manner of their composition." This has been strongly recommended in Smith's Biblical Dictionary, and copied very largely by Dr. S. Davidson. Of this the famous Henry Von Ewald published a critique in his Jahrbuch for 1852-3, pp. 239—244, which begins thus : " This essay of Hupfeld suffers from all the defects in which he has learned to delight . . . The doubts (about the flood) are mere conceits (griller): but the conceit (crotchet) to defend through thick and thin, as the height of wisdom, the views which De Wette entertained in 1807, and which lead necessarily to the conclusions of Bohlen, Strauss, and all that class of pernicious theologians, is really too bad. . . . If Hupfeld in the present day wishes to be a De Wette of 1806-7, or a Bohlen, or a Strauss, then let him; but let him not presume to boast of his love of science, or even of respect for historical truth or fidelity. But when he speaks of the Brussels physician, Astruc, who in spite of all his mistakes, was nearer to the truth 100 years ago, he ought rather to remember that the vulgar herd of theologians, as they now exist in Germany, and to which, according to many signs, Hupfeld himself belongs, have just the same disposition as those in the days of Astruc, to talk nonsense and think falsehood. Hupfeld is in all things, so far as one can judge, far behind the results of science ; but far from being modest on that account, he endeavours with silly words to bring science to nought. Names and notions like ' The Elohist,' ' The Jehovist,' ' The ground document,' in the present day are far beneath all science."

When the first volume of Hupfeld's Psalms appeared, Ewald received it in the same style, and says : " Competent judges could guess from his earlier and smaller works, that he would never produce any thing beneficial either to science or Christianity. Experience of what he has done leads to a more unfavourable judgment. ... To Oriental learning the author can make no pretensions ; and as to the Hebrew language, his knowledge of it is in the highest degree unsatisfactory and incorrect [1]." " But as he does not understand the language and connexion of the Psalms, so he entirely mistakes their historic sense [2]." Ewald gives instances to prove his assertions, very interesting to read, but too long to transcribe. Hupfeld's opinion of Ewald is of the same character; he pronounces Ewald's criticisms and interpretations as untrustworthy. In the preface to the first volume of his Commentary on the Psalms, Hupfeld first makes known his malignant hatred of Hengstenberg, then his reasons for rejecting Hitzig's interpretation, and, lastly, his judgment concerning Ewald. " Ewald's failing is of an opposite character. With equal natural qualifications and conditions for successful research, and with a wider and more striking compass of learning and literary activity . . . it prevents him from being a successful interpreter. ... Finally, his immeasurable self-conceit, which imagines that in his numerous writings he has revealed nothing but irrefragable truth ; and

[1] 7tes Jahrbuch, pp. 137, 138.
[2] 9tes Jahrbuch, p. 168.

whereas,—notwithstanding all the admiration
which has been offered him (and which is specially awarded to half-truths), and all the forbear-
ance which the German public exercises towards
authors who impose on (imponere) them with
bombast, want of taste, and the greatest impro-
prieties—he has not found so much blind faith
as he claims, and has even met with opposition,—
he is not ashamed to ascribe this to enmity to the
truth [3]," &c.　It is sad to find men of learning
speaking with this acrimony of each other.　But
at a time when their authority, especially that of
Hupfeld, is now being obtruded on the English
public, it is well to know what these liberal
divines think of each other, and to be aware of
the fact, that the German school of theology is
far from being that happy family described by
Professor Jowett and others, and that the talk
about their agreement in the main results is
mere talk, the result of ignorance.　D. C. will
hardly ask the English public to accept what he
himself has rejected, or to believe in his supe-
riority to Ewald, Hupfeld, and Knobel, and accept
two authors.]

What they affirm to have been written by two,
three, four, five, six, or more writers, D. C. says
was written by two; and lastly, D. C. is not sure
of his own ground.　In paragraph 214 he says,

---

[3] Pp. xix. xx.

" We shall find that the Elohistic narrative forms
the basis of the whole story from Gen. to Joshua,
fragments of it appearing here and there throughout." Whereas, in § 344, he expresses his belief
that " there is very little in the Pentateuch after
Ex. vi., which really belongs to the Elohist."
To which of these two statements are we to give
credit? or can we at all rely upon a critic who
makes such sweeping and contradictory statements? or will any person, devoid of Hebrew,
but possessed of common sense, where such great
Hebraists differ, trust to his own conclusions,
derived simply from the English Bible? And
yet this is what D. C. invites him to do, and
assures him that if he will only take the English
Bible, and observe " the distinctive marks of the
two writers . . . and remember that the words
'Elohim' and 'Jehovah' are represented in the
E. V. by God and LORD respectively," . . . " he
will very soon arrive at such a conviction of the
reality of the main result of this criticism, as will
decide the question in his own mind for ever."
(par. 469.) Here is criticism made easy [4]. And yet
in the very next paragraph he admits that " *In
a matter so difficult and intricate as this*, it is of
course not surprising that there should still be

---

[4] How slender D. C.'s idea of the qualifications necessary for a critic! Just imagine a young gentleman or lady
undertaking to decide upon the integrity of the Iliad, or the
correctness of Wolf's criticism, by reading Pope's Homer!

difference of opinion among critics, with respect to some matters of detail."

So that D. C. would persuade persons totally ignorant of Hebrew that they can arrive at certainty, where the most celebrated Hebrew scholars of the time are in uncertainty and totally opposed to each other, and where he himself is still wavering and undecided. But, says D. C., it is only in details that they differ. But is D. C. ignorant that the accommodation of details is the very first condition of accurate criticism, and the proof of the competence of the critic and the correctness of the criticism? Or does he call it a trifling matter of detail, when he says there are only two writers in the Penta-teuch, and Ewald says there are seven; when the Bishop therefore affirms that there are only two differences of style, and the German pro-fessor says there are seven? Or is it a trifling matter of detail when the Bishop himself says in one place that the Elohist can be traced to the end of Joshua, and in another that there is very little of the Elohist to be found after Exod. vi.? Or is it a trifling difference of opinion when one learned German asserts that the documents were written before Moses, another that they were written in the time of David, and a third that they were written in the days of Josiah? Would any classical scholar think that it was an in-significant difference if one critic asserted that the false Decretals were written in the days of Augustus, another in the days of Augustin, and a third that they were the product of the 9th century? Would any English scholar trust in the criticism which asserted that the Beggar's Petition was written in the time of William the Conqueror, in the days of Wycliffe, or in the time of Pope and Addison? Would any one believe for a moment that critics making these assertions were in the main agreed, or would he trust in those critics who cannot distinguish between the Latin of the time of Augustus, or Augustin, or the 9th century, or the English of the 11th, the 14th, or the 17th centuries; and yet this is what D. C. seems to think sound criticism. In paragraph 470 he says, "The reader would find no strong marks of distinction in style between the parts of the story supposed to be due to these two Elohistic writers. *It will be sufficient*, however the case may be in reality, that he should for the present at all events regard the Elohistic matter as due to one single hand," i. e. to come to a correct conclusion as to the component parts of the Pentateuch, you may begin with an innocent falsehood that a document written by two different authors was only written by one, and from these false premises you will arrive at a true and correct conclusion; that is, you may believe that parts of Hamlet were written by Beaumont, other parts by Fletcher, and yet come to a right conclusion as to the authorship of that tragedy.

This lax and uncertain method of criticism is sufficient to discredit all D. C.'s criticisms. At first he speaks at large of the whole Pentateuch, then he contracts his dimensions, and instead of the Pentateuch applies his Elohistic Jehovistic theory to Genesis only. Concerning Genesis, not the Pentateuch, he thus writes in paragraph 210:—

"It will be seen hereafter, when we proceed to examine critically the whole book of Genesis, that throughout the book the two different hands which we have already detected are distinctly visible."

How then are these "two hands" to be distinguished? what are the criteria of separate authorship? In reply, D. C. gives several, to be considered in order, of which the first and chief is this:—

"One of the writers, it will be found, is distinguished by the *constant* use of the word Elohim, the other by the intermixture with it of the name Jehovah, which two words in English appear as God and LORD (not 'Lord,' אֲדֹנָי) in our English translation. Sometimes the latter writer uses *only* Jehovah for considerable intervals, as the other uses only Elohim; thus in i. 1— ii. 3, we have only Elohim thirty-five times, in xxiv. only Jehovah nineteen times. Can any

one believe that these two passages were written
by one and the same writer?"

That he here makes the peculiar use of the
two words Jehovah and Elohim decisive is plain
from his reference to two passages of Scripture,
Gen. i. 1—ii. 3, where Elohim occurs thirty-five
times, and, xxiv., where Jehovah occurs, as he says,
nineteen times exclusively, and concludes that
these two portions cannot be written by the
same writer. Let us then examine this argument, premising, first, that D. C. is unhappy in
his choice of these two passages, for in chapter
xxiv., though Jehovah occurs nineteen times as
he says, he is mistaken in saying that in that
chapter "we have only Jehovah nineteen times."
An attentive reader will find that in this chapter
Elohim occurs as well as Jehovah, and that it
occurs six times, namely, in verses 3, 7, 12, 27,
42, 48. So far, therefore, as these two portions
are concerned, his premises are false, and therefore his conclusion untrue. And this inaccuracy
ought to convince the English reader that D. C.'s
statements, even as to matter of fact, are not to
be received on trust, but require verification.
But suppose that his statement here were accu-
rately true, and that in one place there is only
Elohim, in the other only Jehovah; will this
really prove that there must be two writers?
Is it impossible that the same writer might have
had reasons for using Elohim in one place and

Jehovah in the other? D. C. himself shows
that David in the Psalms, written in the later
period of his life, has done just the same,—has
in some Psalms employed Elohim exclusively,
and in others Jehovah exclusively. Thus in
§ 359, when speaking of the eighteen Psalms ascribed to David in the second Book, he says:—
"They include also three from the *middle*
part of his life, Ps. lx. (E. 5. J. 0.) when 'Joab
returned and smote of Edom, in the valley of
salt, twelve thousand men,' in the *forty-fifth* year
of David's life,—Ps. li. (E. 6. J. 0.) after his
adultery with Bathsheba in the *fiftieth* year, and
lxxii. (E. 3. J. 1.) or rather (E. 1. J. 0.) since
ver. 18, 19, are merely the doxology (228)
added by the compiler . . . . and if written by
David, may have been composed by him, shortly
after Solomon's birth, in the *fifty-first* or *fifty-
second* year of his life." Here then are three
Davidic Psalms which employ Elohim only.
Subsequently he admits, § 444, that Ps. ii. "may
have been written in the last years of his life:"
—Ps. cx. "towards the close of his life"—
(§ 447)—Ps. cxxxviii. (E. 0. J. 6.) "in his old
age." Here then are six Psalms, three entirely
Elohistic, three exclusively Jehovistic, and yet he
admits that they may all have been written by
David. If then the same person could have
written these six Psalms, why could not the
same person have written Gen. i. 1—ii. 3. and

Gen. xxiv.? or what is more important still, why could not one person have written the 1st and 2nd chapters of Genesis, though they relate to the same subject? It is only what David has done with regard to one of the gravest incidents of his life—his repentance on account of adultery and murder. D. C. admits fully that Ps. li. relates to that event, and does not deny what the great majority of commentators, ancient and modern, including Ewald and De Wette, affirm, that Ps. xxxii. refers to the same happy humiliation; and yet Ps. li. is exclusively Elohistic, and Ps. xxxii. exclusively Jehovistic. If then David, in two Psalms, written about the same time, in reference to the same event, has in one Elohim only, and in the other Jehovah only, why may not Moses have written some passages entirely Elohistic, others entirely Jehovistic? If the peculiar use of Elohim and Jehovah does not make two authors in those two Psalms, why should it make two authors in Genesis? As David may have had his reasons for the alternation, so may Moses. The truth is, this mode of criticism will prove that Milton did not write the Paradise Lost, nor Samson Agonistes; or if he wrote any of the former he wrote only three out of the nine books. In his Paraphrases on certain Psalms, he uses the words Jehovah and Lord freely and frequently. It is certain, therefore, that he knew the word, and that it was

well known and familiar in his time; and yet
there are nine books of the Paradise Lost, in
which the word Jehovah does not occur at all.
It occurs twice in the first book and once in the
seventh.   In like manner the word "LORD" for
Jehovah occurs only once in the fifth book, and
once in the twelfth book—and perhaps once in
the tenth.   Hence, on D. C.'s principles, we
might contend that the Paradise Lost could not
have been written by the same author who wrote
the Paraphrase to the Psalms, or that only the
books which have Jehovah and LORD are those
written by Milton, and that the other books
were written at an earlier period; before or at
the beginning of the revival of Hebrew learning.
D. C. and his friends will reply,—But we do not
depend merely upon Jehovah and Elohim, we
refer to differences of style, to words and phrases
used in one document and not in another.   He
who asserts that Milton did not write eight
books of the Paradise Lost, perhaps not any,
can also say the style and diction in the books
which have Jehovah, is perfectly different from
that of those books in which it does not occur.

   That there are reasons why Elohim should be
preferred in one case, and Jehovah in another,
will be seen hereafter.   In the meanwhile it will
be sufficient to remark, that D. C. himself admits
that there may be a reason for such preference.
In § 206 he observes, that in Gen. ii. iii. the

words Jehovah Elohim are always used in speaking of the Divine Being, "except in iii. 1. 3. 5, where the writer seems to abstain, for some reason, from placing the name 'Jehovah' in the mouth of the serpent." Here he admits that the same writer had a reason for using Elohim in one place, and Jehovah Elohim in the other. This admission invalidates his criterion of two documents and two writers. It shows that the use of Elohim in one place, and Jehovah in another, is not a proof of two authors, but of different reasons in the mind of one author for the choice of his language. Here in the midst of a passage, which Colenso regards as one of the most striking Jehovistic, four verses, 2—5 of the 3rd chap., of Genesis are Elohistic; and yet he believes that they were written by the Jehovist. The criterion of the names, therefore, is not decisive. The one author had a reason for making these four verses Elohistic, and the rest of the chapter Jehovistic. The same, or similar reasons, may have made the one author use Elohim exclusively in chap. i., and Jehovah Elohim exclusively in chap. ii. and iii.[5]

---

[5] "But that any one, blinded by external appearance, should have derived from a Jehovist a passage in which once or twice the word יהוה was found, or (the assumption) that a chapter, in which the other name occurred, an Elohist must have written, can be explained only on the supposition that they never marked the real difference of these

The first real attempt at a proof of his theory
D. C. gives in § 203, and following paragraphs.
He says, " We will notice the contradictions
which exist between the first account of the
creation, in Gen. i. 1—ii. 3, and the second
account in Gen. ii. 4—25." . . . . And again,
§ 205: " the following are the most noticeable
points of difference between the two cosmogonies."
His first error here is the assumption that there
are two cosmogonies, or two independent accounts
of creation.　Chap. ii. cannot, with any regard
to what it contains, and what it omits, be called
a cosmogony at all.　There is only a passing
allusion in verse 4 to the creation of the heavens
and the earth.　It notices not the creation of the
light, nor the firmament, nor the sea, nor the
dry land, nor sun, moon, or stars, nor fish, nor
reptiles.　It cannot, therefore, be an account of
creation, nor in any sense a cosmogony.　The
first chapter is an account of creation, for it
supplies all that the second chapter omits.　As
therefore the first chapter is, and the second
chapter is not a cosmogony, differences in the
narrative are not necessarily contradictions.　The
author of the second chapter without doubt, as
is admitted, had the first chapter before him,
and would therefore not repeat what was already

two words, probably quite looked upon the one name as
later, and thus invented new opportunity for new theories."
—Ewald, Einleit. (comp. of Gen.) p. 39.

fully recorded in it, but allude only to what was necessary to his own purpose.

That purpose was, as is evident to every reader, to give an account of man's original happy state, and the mode in which he fell into the present state of evil and sorrow. The second chapter refers to the first, and is the necessary preparation for the third. The one cannot be separated from the other; and it is impossible to give a fair criticism or accurate interpretation of the second chapter, if the third be not kept steadily in view. D. C.'s second assumption is that these two chapters contain two independent narratives, and that verse 4 of chap. ii. belongs to, and is the beginning of the second. But this he ought to have proved. He knows, as appears from his reference to "The Aids to Faith," that the question whether this verse belongs to the first narrative or to the second, is one of the most vexed questions of Biblical criticism. Many distinguished Biblical scholars, of the unorthodox as well as of the orthodox party, consider it the end of the first narrative. D. C. considers it the beginning of the second independent narrative, but has not even attempted to answer the formidable objections against this theory. The verse begins with the words "These are the generations of the heavens and of the earth;" and yet in what follows, there is, as has been observed, nothing about the heavens, firmament,

c 2

sun, moon, or stars, and nothing about the earth
as a whole, but only about paradise; and therefore the words, "These are the generations of
the heavens and of the earth," cannot refer to
what follows.   On the contrary, they are exactly
suitable as a conclusion to what had been related
in the first chapter, the creation of the heavens
and the earth; and the pronoun "these" may,
according to Hebrew usage, refer as well to what
goes before as what follows after.   See Gen. x.
20. 32, and xxxv. 26.   It was the duty of D. C.,
therefore, to have entered on this question, and
discussed the objections to his theory.   This he
has shirked, for it requires time, deliberation,
and accurate acquaintance with the Hebrew
text.   This assumption without proof shows
weakness.

Having passed by this difficulty, D. C. pro-
ceeds with what he considers the contradictions
between the two accounts.   The first is thus
propounded, § 205.

I. *Objection.* "In the first (account) the
earth emerges from the waters, and is therefore
saturated with moisture, i. 9, 10.   In the second
the whole face of the ground 'requires to be
moistened,' ii. 6."

Answer. A glance at the verses to which D. C.
refers, answers this imaginary difficulty.   "And
God said, Let the waters under the heavens be
gathered into one place, and let the dry land

appear, and it was so; and He called the dry
land earth." There is not one word of the earth
being saturated with moisture. But it must
have been, says D. C. To which we reply, not
according to the mind of the author. He relates
that God said, "Let the dry land appear, and
it was so." According to his mind, therefore,
when the waters were gathered to one place, the
earth appeared as dry land, and could not therefore be saturated with moisture, for that would
not be dry land. Indeed, the Hebrew יַבָּשָׁה, not
יְבֵשָׁה, means very dry land, being in the intensive
form, and entirely excludes the idea of moisture.
As therefore, according to the historian's view,
the land appeared absolutely dry, it would
naturally require moisture. How that moisture
was obtained, we are told: ii. 6, "There went
up a mist from the earth, and watered the whole
face of the ground." There is therefore no contradiction between i. 9, 10, and ii. 5, 6.

II. *Objection.* " In the first (account) the
birds and beasts are created before man, i. 20.
24. 26. In the second, man is created before
the birds and beasts, ii. 7. 19."

Answer. This objection assumes that the
second chapter relates events in their chronological order, one after the other. But this
assumption is contrary to fact. The historian
alludes to events as they bear upon the object
which he has in view, as is clearly proved by

verses 8, 9, where we read: "And the Lord God planted a garden eastward in Eden, and there He put the man whom He had formed. And out of the ground made the Lord to grow every tree that is pleasant to the sight, and good for food; the tree of life also in the midst of the garden, and the tree of knowledge of good and evil." According to the order of events as here narrated, one would suppose that the Lord first placed man in the garden, and then caused all the trees to grow; whereas, verse 15 proves the contrary, that the trees were first caused to grow, and when they and the streams of water were all ready, "Then the Lord God took the man and put him into the garden, to dress and keep it," and gave him leave to eat of all these existing trees except one. The historian, therefore, does not observe the chronological order of events, but mentions them as they suited his purpose. In like manner, he mentions the creation of the beasts, after he had spoken of the creation of man, because his primary object is not to relate the creation of beasts; but he only mentions them, because the mention of them was necessary to what follows, to shew that it was by naming the beasts that Adam found out his want of a help meet for him, and how that want brought about the creation of woman, who is a main personage in the history of the fall. With the first chapter before him, as it certainly was, he knew the chronological order as well as D. C. himself. There can, therefore, be no contradiction. In the first chapter the creation of the beasts forms an integral part of the narrative, and is therefore related at the right time. In the second chapter it is only alluded to incidentally, as necessary to introduce the account of Adam's sense of his want of a consort, and is therefore related just before the creation of Eve.

III. *Objection.* " In the first (account) all the ' fowls that fly ' are made out of the waters, i. 20. In the second, the ' fowls of the air ' are made out of the ground."

Answer. This is a gross blunder, arising out of D. C.'s neglect or ignorance of the Hebrew text. Chap. i. 20 does not say that the fowls were made out of the waters. The English version is somewhat obscure, and looks like what D. C. says. The Hebrew text is clear and explicit. The English version says : " And God said, Let the waters bring forth abundantly the moving creature that hath life, and fowl that may fly above the earth, in the open firmament of heaven."

Here it looks as if " fowl " was an accusative governed by " bring forth," but in the original it is a nominative, in an independent sentence. " Let the waters swarm with moving creatures, and let fowl fly above the earth." The Hebrew says nothing about what the fowls were made of.

It does not even say that they proceeded from the water. It merely says, "Let the waters swarm with fish and creeping things, and let fowls fly in the air." The English verb "bring forth" may be used of fowls; but the Hebrew verb "Sharatz," swarm, may not be so applied. It is used only of aquatic animals and creeping things; and once figuratively of the Israelites to express their extraordinary increase in Egypt. This objection, therefore, is only a proof of the precipitancy with which D. C. lays hold of anything that appears to cause a difficulty.

IV. *Objection.* " In the first (account) man is created in the image of God, i. 27. In the second, man is made of the dust of the ground, and merely animated with the breath of life; and it is only after his eating the forbidden fruit that 'the Lord God said, Behold the man has (is) become as one of us, to know good and evil,' ii. 7; iii. 22."

Answer. In the first place the relation that man was made of the dust of the ground does not contradict any thing said, i. 27. The first chapter does not say what man was made of, but merely that he was made. The second tells us the material of which he was made. But this is no more a contradiction than if a statuary were to write and say that he had finished a statue of some distinguished personage, and in a subsequent communication say, that it was made of bronze or marble. In the next place, if by the words, "merely animated with the breath of life," D. C. means that Adam was a mere animal or living creature until he partook of the forbidden tree, he can hardly have read the chapter attentively, or duly considered what is there related. The narrative throughout exalts Adam above all other creatures. In the first place he is placed in the garden to dress and keep (guard) it. In this commission it is necessarily implied that he is an intelligent being worthy and capable of trust. In the next place he is described as a free, moral, and responsible agent. God gives him a law—he is not to eat of the tree of the knowledge of good and evil; and this law is accompanied by the awful sanction of death for disobedience. According to this he knew what was right and what was wrong. This alone would place him far above all other earthly creatures. In the next place, the animals are brought to him to be named, and whatsoever name he imposed, that was their name. This implies dominion, even that which is described, i. 26, "Let us make man in our image, after our likeness, and let them have dominion over the fowl of the air, and over the cattle, &c." Adam, then, is here described as intelligent, free, moral, lord over other creatures. Is not this to be like God, to have the stamp of His likeness? Is not this to be more than a mere living creature? D. C. himself, I think, would not deny this conclusion. But then, there is another point still, a feature which distinguishes Adam from all other living creatures. Into Adam's nostrils alone God breathed the breath of life. If the Lord breathed into his nostrils the breath of life, נשמת חיים, it must have been a Divine breath, constituting him not only a living creature, but an intelligent, holy creature, as Elihu says in Job xxxii. 8, referring to this very passage, " Truly there is a spirit in man ; and (rather, *even*) the breath (נשמת) of the Almighty giveth them understanding " (literally, causeth them to understand). D. C.'s insinuation, therefore, that until Adam ate of the forbidden tree, he was a mere animal, and became like God, knowing good and evil only by transgression, is contradicted both by the letter and the spirit of the narrative. The second chapter describes the same nature of man, and ascribes to him the same prerogatives as the first, and still more clearly by giving the particular features of the Divine image which he possessed. But though in some respects like his Creator, as creature there were necessarily other particulars in which he was not like Him. He was not eternal, nor Almighty, nor omniscient. The Creator, by His omniscience, even before creation, even from all eternity, knew good and evil. Adam's understanding being finite, and his nature pure and holy, knew it not. There was therefore an element of truth in Satan's suggestion, that by knowing good and evil, they should become like God. By perseverance in obedience, they might have acquired that knowledge in time innocently. God might have revealed the fall and punishment of Satan, and thus made known the difference between good and evil. By disobedience they obtained in their own persons a guilty and calamitous knowledge, which in one sense made them like God, but practically defaced that glorious image in which they had been created, and made them unfit to be immortal. Fallen man immortal would have become a fiend, and this earth a habitation of devils. Therefore God says, not in irony [6], but in pity, " The man is become as one of us, to know good and evil; and now lest he put forth his hand, and take also of the tree of life, and eat and live for ever. Therefore the Lord God sent him forth from the garden of Eden;" *i. e.*, paraphrased, if he eat of the tree of life and live on, immortal, he will be like his tempter, lost for ever. He must therefore be removed from the possibility: go forth, and toil and die, and thus be brought to feel the unhappy change, which the guilty knowledge of good and evil has brought upon him.

V. *Objection.* " In the first, man is made Lord of the whole earth, i. 28. In the second, he is

---

[6] Comp. Delitzsch. on Gen. p. 194. "Irony concerning an unfortunate misguided soul,—Richers very justly observes,—Satan probably entertains, but not the Lord."

merely placed in the garden of Eden to dress it
and keep it, ii. 8. 15."

Answer. In the first account God speaks of
man as of. the whole human race, and of that
dominion which the race was to acquire, as is
evident from the words, "Be fruitful and mul-
tiply, and replenish the earth and subdue it, and
have dominion over the fish of the sea, &c."
The words cannot be confined to Adam and Eve,
who could not accomplish all this themselves.
The words, "Dominion is given," refer to the
race of man, to mankind, and so David inter-
prets them in the 8th Psalm. The 2nd chapter,
on the other hand, relates that the individual,
Adam, was placed in and over the garden of
Eden. At the same time his dominion over
other creatures is implied in the fact that they
were brought to him to do him homage, and
from him to receive their names, and whatsoever
he called them, that was their name. There is
therefore no contradiction whatever. In the
first chapter we have the prerogative of the
race; in the second, the particular commission
given to the individual.

VI. *Objection.* " In the first, man and
woman are created *together*, as the closing and
completing work of the whole creation, created,
as is evidently implied, in the same kind of way
also, to be the complement of one another; and,
thus created, they are blessed together, i. 28.
In the second, the beasts and birds are created

between the man and the woman. First, the man is made of the dust of the ground; he is placed by himself in the garden, charged with a solemn command, and threatened with a curse if he break it; then the beasts and the birds are made, and the man gives names to them, and, lastly, after all this, the woman is made out of one of his ribs, but merely as an help-mate for the man, ii. 7, 8. 15. 22."

Answer. First, a careful examination of the language of Gen. i. 26—28, shows that according to its author's mind, man and woman were not "created together," i. e. simultaneously [7]. In verse 26 we read, "And God said, Let us make man (*Adam* without the article) in our image, after our likeness, and let them have dominion, &c." Here the language is indefinite. It refers to the whole human race. But then follows, "And God created *the* man (Adam with the article) in His image, in the image of God created He him; male and female created He them." Here the language is definite, "the man," and in the first half of the verse the pronoun is in the singular number and the masculine gender, "In the image of God created He him." If the author had intended briefly to state that at first only one human being, and that one the male, was created, what other language could he have employed? Then, having spoken in the singular number, and the mascu-

[7] Aids to Faith, p. 230.

line gender, he as briefly but clearly describes
the subsequent distinction into sexes, " male
and female created He them." So that we have
here as well as in the 2nd chapter, the creation
of Adam, the male, first, then the mention of the
two sexes, implying that the woman was created
afterwards; so that on this point, instead of contradiction, we have perfect agreement.

" The plan of this chapter forbad his entering
into the detail of the creation of woman, just as
much as it hindered him from describing the
varieties of herbs or trees, or fowls or fishes, or
of beasts of the earth and cattle. As he merely
says that God created them, so here, after the
mention of 'the man,' he just notices the fact
that God created them male and female; but in
that very notice, he implies that there is some-
thing peculiar, for with regard to fish or beasts
or cattle he does not mention that God created
them male and female . . . . With regard to
man, short as is the notice, he does relate, first,
that 'in the image of God created He him,'
that is one male; and then 'male and female
created He them.'

" Even according to the opinion of those who
make the first and second chapters of Genesis
two accounts, written by two authors, the fifth
chapter was written by the author who wrote
the first chapter (the Elohist as they say). But
in the fifth chapter the creation of one pair only
is plainly implied. ' This is the book of the

generations of Adam. In the day that God created Adam, in the likeness of God created He him; male and female created He them; and blessed them, and called their name Adam, in the day when they were created. And Adam lived an hundred and thirty years,' &c. In all this Adam is one person, and yet the first and second verses are a recapitulation of chapter i. 26, 27, in the very words of those verses. Therefore in i. 27, the author took Adam as one individual male human being, as Knobel fairly admits in his commentary on chap. v. 1—5:—

"Adam is here a proper name, as iii. 17 [a]."

With regard to the second part of the objection, that the 2nd chapter places the creation of the beasts, &c., after the creation of the man, and before that of the woman, it is only a repetition of what is said in the 2nd objection, where I have already answered it by showing that the author in the 2nd chapter does not notice events in their chronological order, but in that order which his object requires.

But it is possible not only to answer objections, but to give some positive reasons in favour of the unity of the two chapters or accounts. In the first place, it has been proved above that the words, " These are the generations of the heavens and of the earth, when they were created," cannot be the title of the following narrative,

[a] Aids to Faith, p. 231.

which says but little about the earth, and nothing
about the heavens. They must, therefore, refer
to some previous account of the creation of the
heavens and the earth, i. e. they must refer to
the first chapter. The diction of this first verse
is plainly taken from i. 1. The same verb, ברא,
is used, the same order, heaven and earth, is
also observed. None but the wilfully blind can
mistake the reference. 2ndly, The remainder
of that verse is also a reference to the preceding
chapter. "In the day that the Lord God made
the earth and the heavens." Here the order is
reversed, because in the first chapter [the arrangement of the earth or dry land, and its gar-
nishment with trees, grass, &c., is first described,
verses 9—13. Then follows the arrangement
of the heavens, the sun, moon, stars, &c. And
therefore in the second member of the 4th verse
of the 2nd chapter, the historian uses the word
עשה, which here signifies "to arrange," not "to
make." As it stands in our version, the last
member of verse 4 is a mere tautological repetition of verse 1. In the original, by the use of
the verb עשה, it refers to the narrative of verse 1.
1st, the creation of the heavens and the earth, as
described verse 1. Then the arrangement of
the earth and the heavens, verses 9—19. 3rdly,
the use of Jehovah Elohim is indicative of authority. In the first chapter the author uses Elohim exclusively. In the second and third
chapters, with a slight exception, he employs

Jehovah Elohim; in the fourth chapter Jehovah exclusively. Now it is admitted on all
hands that the writer of the second and third
chapters also wrote the fourth; and, if he was
not the author of the first, that he had at least
that chapter before him. No one pretends that
the first chapter was written by one author, the
second and third by another author, and the
fourth by a third author; why then did he
insert between the Elohim chapter and the Jehovah chapter a narrative with Jehovah Elohim? The use of the two words together is ex-
ceedingly rare. In other places of the Bible it
occurs, as Ewald says [8], only in prayer, or in the
mouth of a speaker where the object is to mag-
nify and exalt the Divine greatness and majesty,
as Exod. ix. 30. Deut. iii. 24; ix. 26. Josh.
xxii. 22. 1 Sam. vi. 20. 2 Sam. vii. 22. 28.
In prose narrative it occurs nowhere but here
and in Jonah iv. 6. The object of thus insert-
ing it between Elohim and Jehovah is plainly to
show that Elohim and Jehovah are one and the
same; that Jehovah is not merely the tutelar
god of Israel, one god out of many, but the
Deity, the Creator of heaven and earth. He
therefore in this place rightly unites the two
words as belonging to one and the same being.
Jehovah is Elohim, and Elohim, the Creator, is
Jehovah. 4th. In the next place, the narrative

[8] Einleit. p. 93.

D

contained in chapters ii. iii. is absolutely necessary to the following history.   According to the
Elohistic theory, chapter v. follows chapter i.,
and is the introduction to the general corruption
and depravity which brought on the flood. But,
without the account of the fall, this general
corruption of all flesh is inexplicable.   Chap. i.
ends with the assurance that God looked on
every thing that He had created, and behold it
was very good; and then if you omit the second
and third chapters, you come suddenly on the
assertion that all was very bad, how is the
change to be accounted for?   How could that
which God had made very good so suddenly
become very bad, as to require the destruction of
the earth and all that was in it?   How was it
that man, created in the image of God, became
so very and universally corrupt, that only one
family was exempt from destruction?   With the
second and third chapters all is intelligible.
Without them all is inexplicable. These chapters
therefore being so indispensably necessary, prove
the unity of the narrative.

The next difficulty which D. C. finds, demon-
strative as he thinks of two different authors, is
in the account of the flood: in par. 208, he
says, " A similar contradiction exists also in the
account of the deluge, as it now stands in the
Bible.   Thus in vi. 19, 20, we read as follows,—
'Of every living thing, of all flesh *two* of every

sort shalt thou bring into the ark, to keep them alive with thee. They shall be male and female. Of fowls after their kind, and of cattle after their kind, and of every creeping thing of the earth, after his kind, two of every sort shall come unto thee to keep them alive."

"But in Gen. vii. 2, 3, the command is given thus:—'Of every clean beast thou shalt take to thee by *sevens*, the male and the female; of *fowls* also of the air by sevens, male and female, to keep seed alive upon the face of all the earth.' It is impossible to reconcile the contradiction here observed in the number of living creatures to be taken into the ark, especially in the case of the fowls, of which one pair of every kind is to be taken, according to the first direction, and seven pairs according to the second."

Reply. To this Ewald justly replies that in the first passage in which the Lord tells Noah of the coming deluge, and the ark as a place of safety, He speaks only in general terms rather to indicate that the beasts, &c., were to be delivered than to prescribe their number. He therefore speaks of two of each in order to point out that they must be male and female. But in the second He gives the particular directions, that they were to go into the ark in pairs, of the clean seven pairs, of the unclean only one pair. But here nothing is said of the pairs of creeping things, though they also were to be

saved, because the author had already mentioned
them in vi. 19, 20, a proof that these two commands were not written by two different authors,
but by one author who wrote continuously, and
therefore connects the second command with the
first.

Having thus introduced his theory, and given
some of the arguments in its support, he pro-
ceeds in his second chapter to give some other
reasons.   In p. 213 he says, "Besides the pecu-
liarity in the use of the Divine Name, there are
other differences in style and language which
are found to distinguish the two writers.   Thus
the Elohist uses the expression, שדי אל, *El Shaddai*, ALMIGHTY GOD, xvii. 1; xxviii. 3; xxxv. 11;
xliii. 14; xlviii. 3; xlix. 25, which the Jehovist
never employs [9]."

Answer.   The first passage to which he refers
cannot, on his own principles be Elohistic, for it
contains the word Jehovah.   How the word got
there he promises to tell us in his third part.
Why not tell us at once?   The same is the case
with his second reference.   It is part of a narrative in which the word Jehovah occurs more
than once; see verses 13. 20.   The only way to
get rid of this difficulty is by forcibly divid-
ing the narrative into fragments, asserting that
verses 1—9 belong to one another, and the re-

[9] "How little the mere שדי can prove in poetry is obvious."—Hupfeld, Quellen der Gen. p. 74.

mainder of the chapter to another, which no one
but a theorist would think of doing. The narrative is continuous, and no ordinary reader perceives any break in the connexion. So with
regard to the reference xliii. 14. Knobel [1], the
most distinguished and profound champion of
the Elohistic theory, pronounces chapters xlii.—
xlv. to be decidedly Jehovistic, notwithstanding
the El Shaddai. The reference xlviii. 3. Hupfeld denies to belong to the Elohist, and ascribes
to a writer posterior to the Jehovist. And so
with regard to the last reference xlix. 25, the
word *Jehovah* occurs in the eighteenth verse.
Of all these references, therefore, two are doubtful, being denied by Knobel and Hupfeld. In
the other four the word Jehovah occurs, and
therefore the Jehovist does use the title El
Shaddai, God Almighty, and therefore the assertion that the Jehovist never uses this title is
untrue. This theory is also contradicted by the
fact that in passages which the Bishop considers
as Elohistic the word Jehovah does occur.

Another difference of language said to be
peculiar to the Elohist is thus set forth by the
Bishop. "Again the Elohist uses *Israel* as *a
personal* name for Jacob, xxxv. 21, 22; xxxvii.
3. 13; xliii. 6. 8. 11; xlv. 28; xlvi. 1, 2. 29,
30; xlvii. 29. 31; xlviii. 2. 8. 10, 11. 13, 14.
21; xlix. 2; l. 2, the Jehovist *never.*" Bp. Co-

[1] Gen. pp. 318, 319.

lenso here again is very positive. And yet Hupfeld, a much higher authority, is equally positive
in ascribing all these passages, and the chapters
whence they are taken, to the Jehovist [2]. We
may therefore leave the Bishop and the German
Professor to settle it together. Again, D. C.
says, " the Elohist uses always *Padan* or Padan-
Aram, i. e. 'the cultivated field of the highlands' for the mountainous districts near the
sources of the Euphrates and Tigris, xxv. 20;
xxviii. 2. 5—7; xxxi. 18; xxxv. 9. 26; xlvi. 15;
xlviii. 7, a name which occurs nowhere else in
any other part of the Bible; whereas the Jehovist uses *Aram-Naharaim*, i. e. the highland of
the two rivers, xxiv. 10, E. V., Mesopotamia,
which name also occurs again in Deut. xxiii. 4.
Jud. iii. 8. 1 Chron. xix. 6. Ps. lx. title."
Answer. In the first place, the chapters xxv.
and xxviii. are clearly as much Jehovistic as
Elohistic; chapters xlvi. and xlviii. are, as we
have seen, according to Hupfeld's judgment, also
Jehovistic. D. C.'s theory therefore is not true.
With regard to Aram-Naharaim, the word occurs only once in Genesis, and twice altogether
in the Pentateuch. It is therefore perfectly
absurd to talk of the Jehovist "*using*" Aram-
Naharaim. Besides it is not by any means
clear that by Padan-Aram and Aram-Naharaim,
the author means the same thing. According

[2] See Die Quellen der Genesis, pp. 46, 47. 56 and 65.

to D. C.'s own explanation, Padan-Aram signifies the "cultivated field of the highlands;"
whereas Aram-Naharaim means "the highland
of the two rivers." It therefore includes the
high land between the two rivers, whether cultivated or not. The one author might therefore
use both Padan-Aram when he spoke of a particular portion, and Aram-Naharaim when he meant
the whole of Mesopotamia, and this is just what
is said by Ewald [3]. "Haran signifies a city
situate in Paddan-Aram; but a Nomade rarely
lives shut up in a city; his is the whole land,
and he and his flocks wander in it from one end
to the other. Thus the names of the city and
the land might interchange without any per-
ceptible change of style. But the Book of Genesis makes a still more delicate distinction with
regard to these names; when Jacob departs from
home it is to Haran that he is always said to go,
because he supposes that he will find the family
dwelling in the city [4]; also when he comes near
the gates of the city, it is concerning Haran
that he naturally inquires. It is true that the
name of the land to which he is going is also
mentioned xxviii. 2. 5—7, but only in opposition
to the land of the Ishmaelites, xxviii. 9. But
when Jacob sets out to return to Canaan, then
he leaves not Haran, but Paddan-Aram; for he
flies not from the city, but from the land in the

[3] Einleit. p. 109.   [4] Gen. xxvii. 43; xxviii. 10.

length and breadth of which he had fed his
flocks. But that the author once uses Aram-
Naharaim instead of Paddan-Aram, and does so
immediately in the beginning of the narrative,
xxiv. 10, before he mentions either Haran or
Paddan-Aram, is only a proof that he first speaks
of (in his time) the better known and larger
portion of Aram, and afterwards uses the name
which he found in his sources, and which
afterwards appears to have died out." As Colenso remarks, the word Paddan-Aram "occurs
nowhere else in any part of the Bible," so that
the use of the three expressions, Haran, Paddan-
Aram, and Aram-Naharaim, does not prove
three or two different authors, but only the
accurate knowledge of the one author who wrote
the whole, and therefore D. C.'s conclusion is
erroneous.

After these attempts to prove his Elohistic
theory, D. C. interrupts his argument, and starts
off to consider other signs of a late date, and
does not return to his favourite theory until page
230, "Introduction to the name of Jehovah."
To this then, I proceed, that we may not be
interrupted in the consideration of the Elohistic
and Jehovistic theory.

In chapter viii. par. 294, D. C. quotes the
famous passage in Exod. vi., putting into italics
those words upon which, in his argument, he
mainly depends. "And God spake unto Moses,

and said unto him, I am JEHOVAH. *And I appeared unto Abraham, unto Isaac, and unto Jacob, by the name of God Almighty* (EL SHADDAI): *but by my name* JEHOVAH *was I not known to them,* and I established my covenant with them, to give them the land of Canaan, the land of their pilgrimage wherein they were strangers," and then comments on it thus:

"The above passage cannot, as it seems to me, without a perversion of its obvious meaning ... be explained to say any thing else than this, that the name Jehovah was not known at all to the Patriarchs, but was now for the first time revealed, as the name by which the God of Israel would henceforth be known, distinguished from all other gods.... So Professor Lee admits, who in his Hebrew Lexicon explains the word Jehovah to be 'The most sacred and unalienable name of God, unknown however to the Patriarchs; it is not, therefore, more ancient in all probability than the time of Moses.' But then we come at once upon the contradictory fact, that the name Jehovah is repeatedly used in the earlier parts of the story, throughout the whole book of Genesis. And it is not merely employed by the writer, when relating simply, as an historian in his own person, events of a more ancient date; in which case he might be supposed to have introduced the word, as having become, in his day, after having been thus revealed,

familiar to himself and his readers, but it is put
into the mouth of the Patriarchs themselves, as
Abraham, xiv. 22, Isaac, xxvi. 22, Jacob, xxviii. 16.
Nay, according to the story, it was known not
only to them, but to a multitude of others," &c.

From which he infers that—

"The recognition of the plain meaning of
E. vi. 2—8, such as that quoted from Professor
Lee (a writer of undoubted orthodoxy), would
be enough at once to decide the question as to
the Mosaic authorship of the Pentateuch. If the
name originated in the days of Moses, then he
himself, certainly in writing the history of the
ancient Patriarchs, would not have put the name
into their mouths, much less into those of heathen
men: nor could he have found it so ascribed to
them in an *older* document.   Professor Lee's
view, therefore, would require us to suppose, that
if Moses wrote the main story of the Exodus,
and of his own awful communications with God,
as well as the *Elohistic* portions of Genesis, yet
some other writer must have inserted the Jehovistic passages.   But then it is inconceivable
that any other writer should have dared to mix
up, without any distinction, his own additions
with a narrative so venerable and sacred, as one
which had been actually written by the hand of
Moses.   The interpolator must have known that
the older document was *not* written by Moses, and
had no such sacred character attached to it."

Now in the first place, D. C. here acts un-critically, and to the English reader unfairly. In a controverted passage, he quietly assumes that the English version exhibits the original Hebrew correctly, both as translation and interpretation, and on the English version he founds his whole argument. But he must well know that in the English version, words are put in which are not in the Hebrew, and that these words so inserted, give a sense which he ought to have proved, not assumed. The English version is this, the words in *italics* not being in the Hebrew:

" And I appeared unto Abraham, unto Isaac, and unto Jacob, by *the name of* God Almighty: but *by* my name *of* Jehovah was I not known to them." For the words " *the name of*," in the first member, and the prepositions "by" and " of" in the second member, there is no equiva-lent in the Hebrew. They were inserted by the translators; the translation, leaving these out, would be—

" And I appeared unto Abraham, unto Isaac, and unto Jacob, by (or in) God Almighty: but my name Jehovah, I was not known to them." Now even as this stands, the sense is greatly altered. The point of comparison is no longer the names " God Almighty" and " Jehovah," but the thing, the substance for which these names stand—the Divine character revealed in " God Almighty," and that revealed in Jehovah. This appears still more plainly if we translate according to the common Hebrew usage. The version will then stand thus:

"And I showed myself to (or, let myself be seen by) Abraham, and Isaac, and Jacob, in (as) God Almighty. But (as to) my name Jehovah, I made not myself known to them." In the first place the two verbs vaéra and nodaḡhti (וארא and נודעתי) are in what is called the Niphal, and a frequent signification of this conjugation is to let or make to be done, that which the original verb expresses simply. Thus the verb "to see," in Niphal, can express, "to let or make one's self to be seen." The verb "to know," in Niphal, "to let or make one's self to be known[5]." Thus the Niphal of *Raah*, to see, here in Ex. vi. 3, translated "appear," is in 1 Kings, xviii. 1, translated "Show thyself," as in verse 1, "Go *show thyself* unto Ahab:" in verse 15, "I will surely show myself unto him this day." In like manner the verb Yadaḡh, "to know," here translated "I was known," must sometimes be translated, "make one's self known," as in our English version, Ruth iii. 3,

---

[5] See Gesenius, Lehrgeb. § 68. 2. 6. Ewald's Grammar, 2nd edition, § 240. 2, where he gives as examples נָסַב, נִשְׁבַּע נִבָּא. Professor Lee in the 2nd edition of his Grammar, p. 124, gives as examples, נִכְבַּד, *he showed himself honourable;* נֶאְדָּר נֶאְדָּר, *he showed himself glorious.*

" Make not thyself known unto the man," and
in Ezek. xx. 9, the first person, as in Exod. vi.
3, " I made myself known unto them." Compare also xxxviii. 23. And so Hupfeld correctly
translates Ps. ix. 17 (16), " The Lord hath
made himself known, He hath executed judgment," referring to Ps. xlviii. 4, Isa. xix. 21,
and other passages besides those cited above.
The first part of the verse will, according to
what has been said, stand thus; " And I showed
(manifested) myself to Abraham, to Isaac, and
to Jacob, IN God Almighty." An English reader
will ask what is the meaning of appearing " IN
God Almighty." To which the answer is—This
is a Hebrew idiom, signifying " as or in the
character of God Almighty;" as Gesenius explains in his Lexicon in his article on the pre-
position בְּ, division C. He gives the passage
before us as an example, and translates, " I
appeared unto Abraham in El Shaddai, that is,
as God Almighty; that is, in the character of
God Almighty." He also refers to Isa. xl. 10,
" Lo the Lord will come (in) as a strong one;"
and Prov. iii. 26, " Jehovah shall be (in) thy
hope;" i. e. thy hope. So Nordheim translates
in his Grammar, § 1040. i, 2. c., " And I appeared
to Abraham in (the character of) God Almighty." He also gives the example from Job
xxiii. 13, " He is in one," where the English
version has added " mind." But the meaning

is, " He is one;" or, as Nordheim explains it,
"He is one," that is, "always the same." Knobel,
in his commentary on Ex. vi. gives the same
interpretation. " He appeared to Abraham,
Isaac, and Jacob, existing in El Shaddai, that is,
as God Almighty." Knobel refers to Gesenius,
and also to Ewald, Gram. § 299 (in the 2nd
Edition, above quoted, it is § 528), where the
same translation and interpretation is given.
Bunsen also in his Bibelwerk gives the same
translation : " Und bin erschienen Abraham,
Isaac, und Jacob, als Gott der Allmächtige;
aber nach meinem Namen, Ewige, war ich ihnen
nicht bekannt." (Knobel and Bunsen also agree
as to the translation of the second part. " But
according to my name Eternal (Jahveh) I did
not make myself known.") We now come to
the second member, which stands literally, " But
(as to) my name Jehovah I did not make myself
known to them." Here then בְּ " in " could not
be repeated. It would not do to say, " I revealed
myself to Abraham, &c. as God Almighty, but
as (in the character of) my name I did not
reveal myself." This would be nonsense. As a
person, a character, God Almighty occurs in the
first member : a person, a character, not a name,
is required. And this homogeneousness of comparison is found in the literal translation, " As
to my name I did not make myself known to
them." For the Hebrew word " Name," espe-

cially when applied to God, does not signify
merely a personal appellation, it takes in at the
same time " essence, nature, character," as is
admitted by the most celebrated modern commentators; thus Hupfeld, in Ps. viii. 2 (1),
" 'How excellent is Thy name in all the earth.'
Name here signifies, what ' name;' both noun
and verb signifies throughout the Old Testament, the essence (Wesen) of things. The
essence of God, as it reveals and manifests itself
in the world, and is therefore continually employed when He is called upon, or when He
appears for help or for judgment, as also for His
dwelling and rule amongst men." And again in
Ps. v. 12, " ' They who love Thy name '—as lxix.
37; cxix. 132, similar to ' They that know Thy
name,' ix. 11. It means simply, They who
love, know, seek Jehovah, that is, His servants
(as lxix. 37, it is the parallel to servants), or the
pious: for *The Name of God* stands as expression of His Essence, as every genuine name is
(hence the verb Qara, *to call*, signifies ' *to be* ').
God's Name is that side of the Divine Being
which is turned towards, and revealed to man,
which manifests itself in His Word and deal-
ings, Word and deed."

In like manner De Wette on Ps. v. 12; " The
Name of Jehovah is Jehovah Himself, in as
much as He is known, honoured, praised." So
also Knobel on Isa. xxx. 27; " ' The name of the

Lord cometh from far.' *Name of Jehovah* is Jehovah Himself, yet not absolutely Himself, but so far as He is known and confessed; therefore so far as He reveals Himself and makes Himself known, as, for example, Mighty and Just, which exactly suits this place. Compare chapters xviii. 7; xxvi. 8. Ps. xliv. 6; liv. 3." Knobel's notes on Isa. xxvi. 8 are also worth transcribing. " *The desire of our soul is to Thy name,* that is, the desire of our soul was, that Thou mightest reveal Thyself, namely, as Him, who is called The Mighty, and the Just One, Jehovah." He evidently takes the name for the revealed nature. The same comprehensive use of the word name is found in the words, Abraham, Israel, Jedidiah. " Thy name shall be Abraham, for a father of many nations have I made thee."—Gen. xvii. 5. " Thy name shall be called no more Jacob but Israel; for as a Prince hast thou power with God and with man, and hast prevailed."—xxxii. 28. So of Solomon it is said, " And the Lord loved him, and he sent by the hand of Nathan, and he called his name Jedidiah " (beloved of the Lord).—2 Sam. xii. 24, 25. In each of these cases the name expresses the nature, the characteristic of the individual named. It is in fact a revelation. Abraham is a father of many nations; Israel, a prince with God; Jedidiah, beloved of the Lord. In the same way we might refer to the names, Immanuel, Wonderful, Counsellor, and Mighty God, &c., as expressing the nature, reality, and essence of Him so named. So in Exod. vi.; "As to my name Jehovah I made not myself known." The meaning is, "As to my essence Jehovah I did not make myself known." And this exactly agrees with what the Lord said and did, as described Exod. xxxiii. and xxxiv. Moses desired to see the glory of the Lord. The Lord promised to proclaim His name, which He did, not merely by pronouncing the word Jehovah, but by revealing His attributes. The Lord proclaimed, "Jehovah, Jehovah, God (El) merciful and gracious, longsuffering, and abundant in goodness and truth, keeping mercy for thousands, forgiving iniquity, transgression, and sin, and that will by no means clear the guilty: visiting the iniquity of the fathers upon the children, and upon the children's children, unto the third and fourth generation." Here God Himself says that to proclaim His name is to reveal His nature, when therefore He says, "As to my name Jehovah I did not make myself known to them," the meaning is, I did not make known my nature as Jehovah. Our translators therefore were mistaken when in Exod. vi. 3 they added to the words of the original text, and translated, "I appeared unto Abraham, unto Isaac, and unto Jacob, by the name of God Almighty: but *by* my name JEHOVAH was I not known to them;" and D. C.

is wrong in following the English version instead
of first explaining critically the original words,
and then arguing from that explanation.   The
error of both is, they thought that God Almighty was a name of God, but God Almighty
is not a name of God, and that the point of
comparison was the name *God Almighty* and
the name Jehovah, whereas the point of comparison is the Revelation of God's nature.   He
revealed Himself to the Patriarch by His attributes—God (or rather Strong one) Almighty.
He revealed to Moses and Israel, His nature,
His essences, by explaining the name Jehovah;
iii. 14, " I Am that I Am."   If therefore we paraphrased Exod. vi. 3 slightly, it would be, " I
manifested myself to Abraham, Isaac, and Jacob,
as Strong, Almighty; but as to my nature and
essence, as expressed by the word Jehovah, I did
not make myself known."   It does not, therefore,
in the remotest degree imply that the name
Jehovah was unknown to them, but only that
the meaning of the name Jehovah had not been
revealed to them; and, therefore, this verse de-
cides nothing against the Mosaic Authorship of
the Pentateuch, nor does it involve any contradiction that the historian puts the name of
Jehovah into the mouth of the Patriarchs, or
records that the Lord spoke of Himself, " I am
Jehovah."   The name was known before Moses.
But it was to Moses, at the burning bush, that

its meaning, "I Am that I Am," was first revealed. D. C.'s objection, therefore, resting,
not upon the original text, but upon an erroneous translation, is erroneous also. So far as
Exod. vi. 3 is concerned, Moses may have been
the Author of the Pentateuch. That the name
then was known before Moses is admitted by
Bunsen and proved by Ewald. Ewald speaks
thus: "It might easily occur to some that Moses
must himself have invented the name. But there
are several things which negative such a supposition. Thus the abbreviated name Jah, which occurs only in poetical pieces, and so rarely in the
later Hebrew writings, is found in some of the
most ancient songs[6] and remnants of songs. In
the next place the word has no clear signification
from any root in Hebrew, which is scarcely con-
ceivable, if it owed its origin to Moses or his time.
[If the word Jehovah comes from one root with
hayah, it must be pre-Mosaic, as the sound of
this root under Aramaic influence is havah,
otherwise always hayah.] But the chief fact is,
that though, so far as we know, the name of
no other person of antiquity shows any trace of
this Divine name, yet Jokébed, the mother of
Moses, does. This leads us to think that the
name, formed like Jacob, Jischaq, was already
in use in the time before Moses, as a name of
God, as indeed *all the simple names of God* and

[6] Exod. xv. 2; xvii. 16.

words of doubtful signification belong to the remotest and earliest time, but that formerly it had been found only in the family of the maternal forefathers of Moses. It had been properly the peculiar name of God in this family, as we may imagine the religion of Israelites in the fore-Mosaic time. But that it first received its signification in the congregation through the great Son of the mother of this single family, remains certain '." Here then Ewald gives three substantial reasons for believing that the name Jehovah was known before its meaning was revealed to Moses. 1st. Because it appears in the hymns of the remotest Hebrew antiquity. 2nd. Because it has no direct etymology in Hebrew, but bears the Aramaic stamp, and therefore could not have been invented in the time of Moses in the then condition of the Hebrew language. 3rd. Because it occurs in the name of Moses' mother, *Jochebed*. This entire supposition that it was peculiar to Jochebed's family, and only became general from the time of Moses, is inconsistent with the history. Jochebed was the daughter of Levi. If Levi knew the word Jehovah as a Divine name, it must have been known to his father Jacob and to all his brethren; and if known to Jacob, then to Isaac

---

' Ewald, History of the People of Israel, 1st Edit. vol. ii. pp. 147, 148. See also Bunsen's note to Exod. vi. 3, in his Bibelwerk.

and Abraham. The assertion therefore that the name was invented by Samuel is perfectly absurd.

But D. C. has another argument against the antiquity of the name Jehovah. He says, § 301 et seq., that in the Pentateuch there are only two names compounded with Jehovah, Jochebed and Joshua, whereas there are scores of names compounded with El; from which he infers that the name Jehovah was not known in early times, and that even in the days of the Jehovist it was but little known, else it would have been compounded with the names of men. But to this it may be replied, that there is not in the Pentateuch, or indeed in the whole Bible, one name compounded with Elohim, so that on D. C.'s principle, it might be inferred that the word Elohim was not known to the Hebrews until after the Captivity. But he himself admits that in the Book of Chronicles, names compounded with Jehovah, are found belonging to persons who went down into Egypt, or who lived before the Exodus, § 306, 307. Such are "Azariah, 1 Chron. ii. 8," in the third generation from Judah. Nay, the wife of Judah's grandson, Hezron, who went down with Jacob into Egypt is Abiah, ii. 24, and Hezron's grandson is Ahijah, ii. 25. . . . In short, such names abounded in these early days, according to the chronicler, just as freely as in the later days, from the age of Jacob's

great grandchildren downwards. *Before* that
age, no such names are given even by the chronicler. .... It is scarcely possible to doubt that
the chronicler has simply invented these names."

Answer. First, that the chronicler invented
these names, is a mere assertion without any
proof. What object could there be in inventing
such names? and why should an inventor have
compounded names with Jehovah rather than
with El? Why should he confine his invention
to the time after Jacob? In the Books of Ezra
and Nehemiah there are names compounded
with Jehovah, but they are the exception. In
the later period of Jewish History, this custom
of using names compounded with Jehovah does
not appear to have been general: and therefore
D. C.'s theory does not agree with the practice
of the chronicler's times. Besides the two critics
who have devoted the most attention to the
Books of Chronicles, Movers and Bertheau,
though Rationalists, assert unhesitatingly, that
the genealogies are the relics of genuine documents, and that the Books contain trustworthy
history. Until therefore Colenso proves the
contrary, no weight can be attached to his un-
supported assertion. According to the Chronicles, names compounded with Jehovah were not
unusual in the earliest times, long before the
days of Samuel. Besides, there is the name
Moriah in the days of Abraham himself. D. C.

takes great pains to prove that Hengstenberg's
explanation of the word cannot be true, and also
that Moriah cannot be the place of the sacrifice
of Isaac; but neither of these propositions, even
if proved, which they are not, can invalidate
the fact that the word is compounded of Mori
and Jah. Mori might signify " My teacher is
Jehovah." But as Gesenius remarks, the sacred
writers refer the word to the root ראה, for
כִּרְאִי־יָה. But whatever the derivation, the last
syllable is certainly יָה; so that a name compounded with Jehovah is certainly found in the
days of Abraham. D. C. after attempting to get
rid of Moriah, goes on to prove from the Psalms,
that in the early days of David the name Jehovah
rarely occurs in his earlier Psalms, but becomes
common in his later Psalms, and thence infers
that the name must have been invented about
the time of Samuel, or, as he thinks, probably
by Samuel himself. Now, without dwelling on
the extreme improbability of such a supposition,
it is to be remarked, that the word Jehovah is to
be found in some of David's earliest Psalms, as in
the 8th Psalm: and, as I have already shown,
David at the same period of his life, wrote some
Psalms exclusively Elohistic, others exclusively
Jehovistic, when he was as well acquainted with
the one word as with the other; so that it cannot
be inferred because he sometimes uses Elohim
exclusively, that he did not know the name

Jehovah, or that it was less familiar than the other.   Indeed, the fallaciousness of arguing from the absence of the name Jehovah, that it was unknown, and that the Book where it is omitted is the more ancient, is proved by the Book of Ecclesiastes. There the name of Jehovah does not occur at all; and therefore on D. C.'s theory, the Book must have been written by an Elohist long before the time of Solomon,—and still more by the Book of Esther, in which no name of God occurs, neither El, Elohim, Shaddai, Jehovah, or any other, from which D. C. ought to infer that this must be the most ancient Book in the Bible.

So far in merely answering objections, but there is one strong positive argument to show that the word Jehovah was in common use in the wilderness.   There are laws which the most determined Rationalists admit to have been given in the wilderness, in which the name Jehovah occurs more frequently. Bleek (in his Einleitung, p. 182-3) lays down certain principles, whereby to distinguish those laws which were actually written by Moses, from those that were only ascribed to him, but really written at a later period. He says, first, if the laws refer to later customs, or to circumstances such as existed after the Israel-ites took possession of the land, they cannot be Mosaic. "But on the other hand, if we find laws which have not the least relation to later times after Moses, but only to a state of things such as existed in the days of Moses, and never afterwards, we have the highest probability that these laws derive from Moses, not only as to the contents, but also were written in the very form in which the Pentateuch has handed them down to us by Moses, or at least in his times. Of such laws, which thus show plain traces of the Mosaic age, there are many especially in Leviticus, but also in Numbers and Exodus; namely, such laws as refer to conditions and circumstances as existed only whilst the people wandered about in the desert, and had their habitations crowded together in a camp and tents, as was the case in the days of Moses, but which afterwards entirely changed when once the people were established in the possession of the land, and had spread themselves about in cities and in the country. An example of this kind is presented to us in Leviticus by the series of laws with which this book begins, that is, in chapters i.—vii., the directions concerning the various sorts of sacrifices . . . . the references to the locality are always to the camp and the desert, which are here presupposed. Thus in chapter iv. 11, 12 (in the law concerning the bringing of a bullock if the priest sin in ignorance) it is said, ' And the skin of the bullock, and all his flesh, with his head, and with his legs, and his inwards, and his dung, even the whole bullock shall he carry *forth with-*

out the camp unto a clean place, where the ashes
are poured out, and burn him on the wood with
fire: where the ashes are poured out shall he be
burnt.' And again, verse 21 (in the case of
the offering for the people), 'And he shall carry
forth the bullock *without the camp*, and burn
him as he burnt the first bullock.' If written
in a later age, these directions could not have
appeared in this form, as then the expression
'without the camp' would have no meaning.
To make these commands practicable in a later
age, a modification, suitable to the altered circumstances, was absolutely necessary. Besides,
in this whole series of laws, the priests are never
spoken of in general terms, but always specially
as, ' Aaron and his sons,' or 'the sons of Aaron,
the priests,' or 'the sons of Aaron the priest;'
see i. 5. 7. 11; ii. 2. 10; iii. 2. 5. 13; vi. 2. 7.
9. 11. 13. 18; vii. 10. 31. 33, 34. This would
scarcely be the case if these laws had not been
conceived in the time when Aaron and his sons
actually presided over the priesthood . . . . A
similar and equally plain example is found in
Levit. xvi. concerning the great day of atonement. This law is connected with the narrative
contained Levit. x. 1, &c., and contains the
direction that Aaron, and the son who should
succeed him in the priestly office, should not
enter into the Holy of Holies within the vail,
except prepared by certain ceremonies, and on

the day of atonement only. But this law is so drawn, that properly, according to the letter, it could only be applied whilst the people of Israel sojourned in the wilderness, and dwelt in a camp. To this condition of things there are the plainest references. Thus where it is said that Aaron should send away one of the two goats into the wilderness, i. e. outside the camp; and again, verses 21, 22, that Aaron should send him away by the hand of a fit man into the wilderness, and the goat shall bear upon him all their iniquities into a land not inhabited, and he shall let go the goat into the wilderness; and again, when in verse 26 it is commanded that the man 'should wash his clothes and bathe his flesh, and then come into the camp;' and again the same command is repeated, verses 27, 28. If this law had been given in a later time, when the Israelites no longer abode in the Arabian wilderness, but in the land of Canaan where they no longer dwelt in camps, but in cities and villages, these directions must have been given in an entirely different form to suit the then existing circumstances. And here also it is not to be forgotten, that this law also is first directed to Aaron; that the high priest is not spoken of in general terms, but mention is every where made of Aaron personally (verses 2, 3. 6. 8, 9. 11. 21. 23), and it is only in the 32nd and 33rd verses that it is pre-

* See in the original German, ' to Azazel,' p. 185.

scribed for the future that the atonement should
be brought by him who had succeeded his father
in the high priestly office." Similar is the law of
leprosy, chapters xiii. xiv.; the purification by
the ashes of the red heifer: and of all these
passages it is certain that they must have been
written in the wilderness; and in all these passages the name Jehovah occurs repeatedly. It
is certain therefore that the name was in common use long before the days of Samuel. Similar
testimonies might be gathered from Joshua and
Judges if there were time, but these we leave
to the reader's own study. It appears that the
name was known before the time of Moses by
the genealogies; and in the days of Abraham, as
is proved by the word Moriah; that it was known
in the days of Levi, as is testified by the ancient
hymns, and by the name Jochebed; that it was
freely used in the desert, and therefore must
have been familiar to the Israelites from that
day forward. The use of the name therefore in
the Pentateuch is not a difficulty, but a proof
that the Pentateuch was written by Moses.

THE END.

GILBERT AND RIVINGTON, PRINTERS, ST. JOHN'S SQUARE, LONDON.